THE
Irresistible
Church SERIES

Engaging Game
CHANGERS

Engaging Game CHANGERS

Recruiting and Coaching
Volunteers for
DISABILITY MINISTRY

by Ali Howard

 THE **IRRESISTIBLE CHURCH** SERIES

Copyright © 2016 Joni and Friends

Engaging Game Changers
ISBN 978-0-9965522-5-7

Author: Ali Howard
Contributing Authors: Rachel Roleder, Gina Spivey, Ryan Wolfe
Collaborators: Karen Roberts, Laura Pulido
Contributing Editor: Mike Dobes
Editor-in-Chief: Marc Stein

Printed in the United States of America.
Scripture quotations are taken from the Holy Bible, English Standard Version®, copyright © 2001 by Crossway Bibles, a publishing ministry of Good News Publishers. Used by permission. All rights reserved.

Produced by The Denzel Agency (www.denzel.org)
Cover and Interior Design: Rob Williams

For information or to order additional print copies
of this and other resources contact:
Joni and Friends International Disability Center
P.O. Box 3333, Agoura Hills, California 91376-3333
Email: churchrelations@joniandfriends.org
Phone: 818-707-5664

Kindle version available at www.irresistiblechurch.org

CONTENTS

Engaging Game Changers

Measuring the impact of volunteers is something that many organizations attempt to do. Volunteers who are faithful, talented and passionate about the ministry with which they serve are worth their weight in gold. Many large nonprofits and countless churches rely heavily on volunteers to accomplish their work and advance their goals. At the time this book was written, Independent Sector, the leadership network for nonprofits, estimated the average value of volunteer time at $23.07 per hour. A church using ten volunteers for three hours a week can save $692.10 per week, $2,768.40 per month and $33,220.80 per year. Volunteers can help facilitate a Sunday morning ministry, assist with administrative tasks, provide manpower at an event, and can even help with the training and management of other volunteers. Speaking in a strictly business sense, these volunteers are game changers, giving the nonprofits and churches they serve the leading edge.

It is easy to see however, that the advantage of utilizing volunteer help goes far beyond dollars saved and tasks accomplished. The *true* impact of volunteers is immeasurable. Recently a church in Southern California decided to bless families in their congregation affected by special needs by inviting them to enjoy a day at the beach. The church recruited enough volunteers that kids could play in the water and along the shore with careful supervision. The parents were able to sit on the beach and simply hang out with other moms and dads who completely understand—without a word of explanation—the difficulties, joys and pressures of having a special needs child. Throughout the event parents had enormous smiles on their faces. Many repeatedly shared, with tears in their eyes, that they felt like they had experienced a slice of heaven by being there that day. One young man who has severe autism and generally only uses about ten words embraced a volunteer and with a beaming smile exclaimed, "Best day ever!" Without all the volunteers who helped to keep the kids safe and happy this kind of experience would never have been possible for these families.

Can you quantify what it means to a family affected by disability to be able to relax and enjoy a

Saturday at the beach like any other family in South ern California? Can you measure the peace and joy that comes from *finally* being able to close your eyes for a moment, wiggle your toes in the sand and feel the sun on your face for the first time in over a de cade without fearing that your beloved child might run away, injure themselves, or get into something they should not? Giving those families a rare oppor tunity to laugh, smile, and be completely themselves is something that cannot be measured.

These intangible, immeasurable elements of vol unteer involvement are the true heartbeat of special needs ministry. This kind of impact is what really makes volunteers game changers. Volunteers are game changers, not only because of the work they accomplish for a very busy ministry, but because of who they are and the influence they have. Begin to think about the volunteers serving in your minis try. Now, ask yourself how you view the role of vol unteers, how volunteers transform the culture of your ministry, and what value you bring to the lives of your volunteers. Are your answers to those ques tions what you expected them to be? Your view of vol unteers will strongly influence ministry support and growth moving forward.

As indicated in the subtitle of this book, engaging game changers is only a portion of the equation—training them and coaching them are also important. Anyone familiar with sports knows that while recruiting the right members of a team is important, coaching the athletes is what really makes a winning team. Recruiting game changing volunteers is important, but training and coaching your volunteers will maximize the effect that you and your entire ministry can have.

We believe that volunteers can help your church become Irresistible—an authentic community built on the hope of Christ that compels people affected by disability to fully belong. This book is designed to encourage ministry leaders to focus on the heart and impact of volunteers while also answering practical questions on how to establish a thriving volunteer program to support your special needs ministry. Engaging game changers is a three-part strategy that includes recruiting, training and coaching. We will take a look at each section of this strategy in the following pages.

Recruiting Game Changers

As you dream of how you want your ministry to operate it is easy to get excited, imagining a fully accessible church (both in facilities and in heart) with plenty of resources and opportunities for families affected by special needs. For many ministry leaders these dreams come to a precipitous juncture as they realize that in order for these dreams to become reality they need help. They need volunteers. Admittedly, volunteers in the church can be hard to come by, but it is certainly not impossible! The recruitment of volunteers entails three primary elements: *how* you ask, *who* you ask, and *what* you ask them.

HELP WANTED - How You Ask

There are as many different ways to ask for volunteer help as there are flavors of ice cream. You could make an announcement from the pulpit or show a short video on Sunday mornings. You could hang flyers in the halls of your church. You could approach individuals one-on-one or connect with community group/Bible study leaders. Your church could host a Disability Awareness Sunday🐚 or hold a disability awareness training event.🐚 With a little creativity, the possibilities are almost limitless! Some methods tend to work better than others, but which method works best largely depends on your unique church and on how much support you have from the pastoral team. My best recommendation is to experiment with multiple methods, allowing you to reach different audiences at different times.

As you strategize how to ask for help in your ministry, we encourage you to spend more time considering the language you use rather than the color of the flyer or the background of your PowerPoint slide.

How often have you heard someone (or yourself) attempt to recruit volunteers for a ministry with something like the following: "Hi, Lisa! We really need some extra hands to help with our Sunday morning disability ministry. Would you be willing to help? I promise it is fun and we have a great time. Don't tell me you are too busy! I think you would be a great fit and it would really bless the rest of our team to have a few more people in rotation." While this sounds like a fair pitch, it is actually communicating a few

🐚 This symbol indicates that there are supplemental resources that correspond with this topic at http://www.joniandfriends.org/church-relations/

things that you may not want to communicate—
1) that you are desperate (even if you are, you do not want to make your appeal out of desperation), and 2) that you do not care who signs up, all you need are bodies in the room.

What if the appeal went something like this, instead: "Hi, Lisa! I was curious if you would be interested in joining our ministry team to serve families of our church affected by disability. You have such a gift with communication and there is a sweet, young girl in our ministry who struggles to communicate. I think you could really bless her and teach her a lot. The commitment would be two Sundays a month for the next six months and we will make sure you are fully trained and equipped to serve in this capacity. These families are so dear to me; I do not want just anyone serving them! But I have watched you with your own kids, and I really think you would be a great fit. Please let me know if you are interested!" This type of appeal will typically get a much better response because it is personal, specific, recognizes the value of the volunteer and communicates that you have a high quality program.

Generally speaking, people are more apt to engage in something that is well organized and somewhere they can make a difference. Before you begin recruiting volunteers take time to organize your ministry and define the roles in which you will need volunteers to serve. If you are unsure of how to start a special needs ministry, I recommend reading the Irresistible Church book *Start with Hello*. Then, as you begin to recruit individuals to serve alongside you in your ministry you can communicate with a specific, personal invitation that will be much more effective. When recruiting volunteers we recommend clearly communicating the details of the volunteer position up front. You can even create a simple position description so that individuals who are interested can see at a glance what serving would entail.

While people are more likely to sign up if they know what they are signing up for, your chances of gaining new recruits increase even more if you can communicate how they can make a difference and that you are excited about your ministry. When ministry leaders apologetically beg people to join their team they are revealing a lack of enthusiasm that will be contagious to all their volunteers. A leader who is proud of their ministry and excited about what God is doing through it will also instill those values in their volunteers.

So, as you begin to strategize how you engage game changers, spend time thinking about how you present your ministry. As a special needs ministry leader, you are engaging in service that is life changing, challenging, rewarding and fun. You are making a tremendous difference in the lives of the families that you serve. You have the potential to bring many to Christ simply by loving them well through your ministry. Be proud of your ministry, be excited about what you do, and set the example for your volunteers—you and your team are engaging in a ministry that can truly change the landscape of eternity.

HELP WANTED - Who You Ask

Many churches that we encounter feel the individuals within their congregations are already overextended by serving in several areas—to ask them to serve in one more capacity would simply be too much to ask. However, upon closer examination, this is rarely as true as it appears. Most churches have a handful of individuals who zealously serve in several areas, but there are also many people in their congregation who have not yet found their niche for serving. Admittedly, accessing these individuals who have not yet found a ministry with which to serve can be difficult.

So, acknowledging that finding volunteers in an active church can be challenging, where can you look to find them?

We encourage you to look to other ministries within your church to find volunteers. You might be thinking, "I can't steal volunteers from other ministries!" Please do not worry! We are *not* telling you to go and steal people away from other ministries, but rather to *partner* with other ministries within the church to provide opportunities for individuals to serve together. You can connect with the leader of the youth ministry to see if he or she would be willing to partner with you to create a buddy system between their students and the friends in your ministry. (Please note: buddies is the name we have given to those who serve within special needs ministry, and friends is the name we have given to individuals who are served by the special needs ministry.) It is probably not wise for students of the youth ministry to serve in the special needs ministry every Sunday, but serving once or twice a month could not only bless the friends in your ministry, but also teach valuable lessons to the students in the youth ministry. The special needs ministry of a local church near Los Angeles uses the rule of thumb "attend one, serve one," allowing the kids in the youth group to serve and to also attend church regularly.

Adult community groups often enjoy serving together. Perhaps you could approach the director of the community groups at your church to see if they will allow you to speak to the group leaders and present them with the opportunity to serve together through your ministry. I previously attended a church in Nashville whose community groups were built with a focus on missions. Each group chose an area of ministry to support—whether it was within the church or outside the church. One group supported the teachers of the underprivileged elementary school where the church met, one group had an emphasis on evangelism and discipleship through daily life, and several groups focused on outreach to a community of refugees who resettled in the Nashville area. Prior to my experience with this church, I never could have imagined the strength of friendship that can come from serving together as brothers and sisters in Christ. This style of community group not only blessed various people groups in the city, but it also brought an amazing closeness in the fellowship that was experienced by serving together as the body of Christ.

Depending on the size and structure of your church and the ministries within your church, you could approach many different groups with this wonderful opportunity to serve together. From the youth to the elderly members of your church, everyone can play a different role. Some volunteers can serve as buddies for friends in your ministry. Other volunteers can help with the administrative needs of your ministry such as scheduling volunteers, coordinating snacks, overseeing the check-in/pick-up process, making sure the paperwork for new families is filled in and filed correctly, and other essential responsibilities.

With the hectic, busy schedules that most of us maintain it is easy to turn everything into a task that can be checked off a list. I encourage you, in the midst of your recruitment, to make an effort to invest in each volunteer that signs up, because passionate volunteers can quickly become an army of recruiters for your ministry. If your volunteers enjoy serving in your ministry and feel appreciated and fulfilled through their time there, they are typically glad to spread the word and invite their friends to come and serve with them.

Tammy was an energetic volunteer for a non-profit in Tennessee. She was so passionate about her work that she not only served the ministry faithfully, but also shared about the ministry with almost everyone she met—her dentist, her stylist, her book club friends, her church family, and many others. As the months went by this ministry began to receive phone calls, emails and donations from new contacts interested in learning more about how to get involved with the ministry. The common thread between all of these new supporters? They had learned about the ministry from Tammy. This volunteer became the best recruiter the ministry had, sharing the vision of the ministry with everyone she met. The reach of the ministry significantly expanded because Tammy was engaged, was excited about her role on the team and understood the impact being made.

We encourage you to look in every area of your church to recruit volunteers, sharing the heart and vision of your ministry as you go. As you ask around, do not be shy to inspire people with stories of families whose lives were changed through special needs ministry. People make time for what they feel is important. If individuals within your church catch the vision of what your ministry is doing you will have an easier time recruiting.

So, as you look for volunteers to serve in your ministry set aside time to connect with the leaders of other ministries within your church to see how you might be able to partner with them. Do not be afraid to ask specific individuals whom you feel would be well suited for your ministry. Ask people who vary in age and talents. And intentionally invest in your volunteers so that they want to invite their friends—this will begin to create a great team of committed game changers!

HELP WANTED - What You Ask

Have you ever signed up to help with something, and when you arrived you stood around for a prolonged period of time waiting for the person in charge to tell you what to do? You probably saw a couple people running around doing things, but you did not really know how to jump in and help. How did that make you feel? You probably felt a bit awkward, in the way, and ultimately not needed. Being unprepared can create more than just a hectic morning; it can create unwanted emotions in your volunteers. One of the best ways to avoid this is to know what you are asking them to do. Before recruiting volunteers, take time to ask yourself the following questions.

- *What specifically do you need help with in your ministry?* Every church functions differently and every ministry within the church has unique needs. Narrowing down what you need and how a volunteer can help fill those needs is a critical piece of building your volunteer program.
- *How many volunteers will you need?* Determine the ideal number of volunteers for each position to create consistency in your ministry but not lead to a feeling of burnout.
- *What training will you provide for your volunteers?* Some churches prefer to do large group training sessions while others prefer to do shadow-style training where new volunteers shadow veteran volunteers, learning as they go. The next section of this book will cover both styles in greater detail.
- *What will happen if a volunteer needs to cancel after you have scheduled them for a shift?* Having a good volunteer substitute plan can save you time and headache.
- *What kind of application/background check will be needed for your volunteers?* This may vary depending on what state you are in and your church's background check policy. Generally speaking,

whatever vetting process your church uses for the volunteers in the children's ministry can be used for volunteer vetting within your ministry.

- *What time frame are you asking your volunteers to commit to?* Determine how many times per month you would like volunteers to serve as well as how many months out of the year. Having this expectation clearly communicated allows volunteers to know what they are signing up for and generally results in stronger commitment levels. For Sunday morning ministry we generally recommend having two buddies assigned to each friend. The buddies would serve every other week giving them a balanced schedule, but also allowing their friend to have a sense of consistency and comfort. Taking into consideration the rhythm of other ministries in the church can allow your volunteers to serve in other areas as well.

- *What kind of ongoing support will the volunteers in your ministry have?* If a volunteer encounters a difficult situation, do your best to provide a place that they can come with questions and concerns. You may also want to consider providing ongoing training opportunities to further equip your volunteers. These training opportunities could be disability ministry specific or could be broader and include topics like communication and leadership.

Once you can answer those questions you will be able to give your recruits a better idea of what serving with your ministry looks like. It can be very helpful to create a position description based on the above information. Position descriptions of this style are generally short, one page documents outlining the basics of the ministry and what is expected of volunteers serving in the ministry. It will also provide a basis of accountability for volunteers should they happen to get "off track" in their service.

Of equal (and possibly greater) importance to all the logistical details of volunteering, a new recruit will probably want to know what impact their service will make. This is really the heart of what you are asking for when you recruit volunteers. You are asking for people who will step outside their comfort zone and give of themselves to share the gospel. You are asking for individuals who are willing to love and be loved in return, to give their time and talents to help the ministry excel. You are asking your volunteers if they will evangelize and disciple one of the most ignored people groups. You are asking people if they are willing to give exhausted parents and caretakers a chance to attend church or have time to rejuvenate. You are asking for volunteers who want to change the world one high five or hug at a time.

You may have noticed a theme throughout this book: While the logistics of your volunteer program are important, the heart behind it is what will really make it thrive. Taking time to think about *who* you ask, *how* you ask, and *what* you ask will give you a strong foundation as you recruit volunteers to serve in your ministry. The theme of focusing on the heart behind volunteering will be woven throughout this book as we continue the discussion of how to train and coach a team of volunteers to become game changers!

Training Game Changers

Training is the part of any discipline (sports, music, art, etc.) that is tedious, hard work with very little glamour. But it is where the foundation is laid and where the rules of the game are learned. Training is a critical component to equipping your volunteers. With proper training volunteers will feel confident to engage in ministry regardless of whether or not they have previous experience serving individuals with special needs.

For a church just starting a special needs ministry, a large group training where many individuals can be equipped simultaneously is a great idea. For churches that have an established special needs ministry, shadow-style training can be very effective as new volunteers join the team. In shadow-style training a new volunteer learns their role over several weeks as they shadow a teacher working with their friend. We recommend making some sort of initial and ongoing training mandatory for volunteers serving with your ministry as all volunteers need to have at least some level of training to be successful in the long run.

In this chapter we will take a look at both types of training. And before you start planning the logistical details of training your volunteers, please take time to pray for them, for the direction of your ministry and for the families you will be serving.

Large Group Training

Large group training is a time of fellowship, fun and learning. New volunteers have the opportunity to meet others who are getting involved with the ministry, and you as the leader have the opportunity to get acquainted with some of your new volunteers. Getting to know your volunteers on a personal level is important because it will help you know where to place each of them most effectively.

The Logistics of Your Training

Getting a day, time and location for your training on the calendar should be done well in advance. This will allow you to get the event on your volunteer's radar early increasing the likelihood of their ability to attend. Coordinate with your church or other facility where you will be holding your training to determine the ideal date. Holding your training before or after church services can be convenient, and if many of your volunteers are parents, hosting it at a time when childcare is already available will make it easier for them to attend.

Designing your training event to be interactive and succinct will keep your volunteers engaged. We suggest holding your training over a time-frame of two and a half hours. If needed, this could also be broken into two hour-long sessions done on two separate days. We encourage you to work hard to complete your training on time or under time as this will communicate to your volunteers that that your ministry is well organized and you value their time.

The Content of Your Training

The content covered in the outline below is a great starting point, but it is certainly not exhaustive. What you include from this list—or what you add to it—will largely depend on the specifics of your church and volunteers.

Volunteer Training Event Outline (2.5 hours)

1. Welcome – 5 minutes
2. Spreading the Vision – 50 minutes
   - Vision and Mission (5 minutes)
   - Creating a Culture of Servanthood (15 minutes)
   - Overview of Your Ministry (5 minutes)
   - Biblical Worldview of Disability (5 minutes)
   - Sharing Christ with an Individual who has Cognitive Delays (10 minutes)
   - Disability Etiquette (10 minutes)
3. Spreading the Vision – 50 minutes
4. Q & A – 10 minutes
5. Break – 10 minutes
6. Behavior Modification – 30 minutes
7. Discussing the Details – 15 minutes
   - Confidentiality (5 minutes)
   - Communication (5 minutes)
   - Policies and Procedures (5 minutes)
8. Closing (10 minutes)

You may notice that the above times total 2 hours and 10 minutes, leaving an extra 20 minutes unscheduled. We have found that it can be helpful to schedule a few extra minutes in case your training runs long. If it runs on schedule you can bless your volunteers by concluding a few minutes early!

In addition to your initial training, you could also hold quarterly or semi-annual trainings for continuing education. At these trainings you can talk more in depth about any of the above topics or invite guest speakers to come and share from their field of expertise. You could invite pastors, therapists, or even parents of children affected by special needs. Inviting these individuals to attend short training sessions can provide your volunteers with practical information and encouragement. Holding follow-up trainings can be a great way to pour into your volunteers and continue increasing their level of expertise. Let's take a closer look at each section of the suggested outline.

Spreading the Vision

Vision and Mission

Forward momentum is difficult, if not impossible, without vision. Take time to share the vision and mission of your church and ministry with your volunteers reminding them that by serving with your ministry they are engaging in disciple making. Helping your volunteers see how the special needs ministry aligns with and complements the overall mission of the church helps them to understand that they are part of a bigger picture.

Creating a Culture of Servanthood

Take time to paint the picture of why your volunteers' efforts matter. There will inevitably be days that are difficult and draining for your volunteers, but if they understand why they are ultimately serving it will give them strength. The primary motivation for serving should be to honor and glorify the Lord through evangelism and discipleship. There is truly no greater calling in life than this! Several Scriptures that compliment this section include Colossians 3:23-24, Matthew 28:19, Mark 16:15, Acts 1:8 and Luke 24:45-47.

A secondary motivation is the blessing that it brings to the families being served by your ministry. This is a great place to share personal stories of families impacted by special needs ministry. You could invite a veteran volunteer to briefly share their experience and the impact that serving has had on them. If your ministry is new, talk with other special needs ministry leaders and ask for stories of the families that they serve. Sharing these stories can inspire and encourage your volunteers.

Overview of Your Ministry

Having an understanding of how your ministry runs will allow your volunteers to serve more effectively. We recommend sharing with your volunteers the various positions that exist within your ministry (buddies, scheduler, snack coordinator, teachers, etc). Explaining the positions will also allow your volunteers to see where they might be best suited to serve. Placing volunteers in their area of strength will lead to greater enjoyment on their part and most likely a stronger commitment to serving. Sharing the leadership structure of your ministry will help your volunteers know who to approach when they have questions. It can also be a great idea to walk through the schedule of a typical Sunday morning or respite event (depending on what you are recruiting volunteers for).

It can also be a good idea to remind your volunteers that, as is true with any ministry, there will be some hard work involved. It will not always be easy and it will often be messy, but if they are willing to engage in the lives of the friends they serve they will be greatly blessed!

Biblical Worldview of Disability

How does suffering fit into God's plan for His people? Can someone with an intellectual disability accept

Christ as their Savior? These and other similar questions are important for you to address as you train your volunteers to be disciple makers with their friends. Biblical characters like Job, Joseph and even Jesus Himself provide us with beautiful examples of the growth and blessing that can come from suffering when we allow God to work in our hearts. Passages like Luke 14, 1 Corinthians 12 and Galatians 3:23-29 emphasize that all people are equal and valued in God's eyes. Regardless of race, gender, abilities or disabilities, God values each of us, and we are to value those around us in the same fashion. The expression of faith may vary between each unique individual, but God calls every person to a saving faith in Him, there are no exceptions. If you would like more in-depth information on this subject we recommend Joni and Friends' *Beyond Suffering* resources. Having a theological understanding of suffering will help your volunteers see each friend in your ministry as a valuable individual worthy of their time and affection.

Sharing Christ with an Individual who has Cognitive Delays

As important as the logistics are for running a special needs ministry, the essential role for every leader and volunteer should be sharing Christ with your friends and their families. Keeping your friend's spiritual growth forefront on your minds and believing they are capable of having a personal relationship with Christ is paramount. Encourage your volunteers to talk with their friends about who Jesus is, what He has done, and how to be saved, at a level their friends can understand using concrete and simple language. Communicating through pictures, yes-no questions and other non-traditional methods can allow your friends the opportunity to acknowledge their understanding and express their faith.

Friendship Ministries (www.friendship.org) has developed a curriculum called *Expressing Faith in Jesus*. It is a great resource that provides practical insight on helping friends with an intellectual disability fully understand the Gospel and communicate their belief in Jesus.

Once the friends in your ministry come to a saving faith in Christ, your volunteers can begin discipling them through their time together.

Disability Etiquette

If you have volunteers who are new to disability ministry they may have some fears and uncertainty about meeting and spending time with their friends. Teaching your volunteers about various types of disabilities and how to interact with people who have these disabilities can greatly ease their nerves. We recommend looking at the Disability Etiquette handout available with this book's online supplemental resources.⬱

One of the easiest ways to exercise disability etiquette is to use "Person-first Language." Person-first Language is talking in such a way that emphasizes the person over the disability; it reminds us to see a person made in the image of God first and their disability second. As an example, using Person-first Language you would refer to a boy who is blind rather than a blind boy.

Engaging your volunteers in a "disability experience exercise" can be a wonderful training tool. This kind of exercise can be done in a short timeframe or extended for several hours. A full description of these exercises and how to set them up can be found in the online resources.⬱ If you choose to use a "disability experience exercise" in your training please remind your volunteers that it is meant to give them a glimpse into what living life with a disability might look like. It should help able-bodied individuals have a better understanding of the friends they serve, but should not be used as an opportunity to feel pity or make light of what they deal with on a daily basis.

Q & A

It may seem strange to include a Q & A session at this point in your training rather than at the conclusion of the event. We suggest holding a time for questions at this point as the topics you have covered so far will be less prone to "rabbit-trailing." The policies and procedures of your ministry covered in the second session can provoke any number of "what-if" scenarios that are generally better answered one-on-one to respect the time of everyone else in attendance. Opening the floor for questions mid-way through your training rather than at the end will also help you conclude the event in a timely fashion.

Break

We encourage you to include a short break allowing your volunteers to stretch, run to the restroom or grab a snack. Having snacks and water available for your volunteers throughout the training is a small way to say thank you for attending. Giving people a short break should help to increase their retention through the second half of the training.

Behavior Modification

Helping your volunteers understand how to navigate behavior challenges is potentially one of the most important things you can teach them during training. All behavior is a form of communication, but if your volunteers do not understand this concept there can be increased risk of frustration and unnecessary escalation. There are basic behavior modification techniques that you can teach your volunteers to help prevent and/or lessen the number of behavior challenges that occur. Friends in your ministry may become anxious or frustrated as a result of things like light, sound, smell and over-stimulation.

Teaching your volunteers to recognize behaviors as communication and providing tips on what to do when their friends become agitated can make a tremendous difference. We suggest basing this portion of your training on real-life scenarios as this will help your new volunteers have a practical understanding of behavior modification. The online ministry resources accompanying this book provide examples of real-life situations you can use to teach these techniques.

Encourage your volunteers not to give up when their friend's behavior feels like more than they can handle. Every individual wants to be heard even if they have difficulty using words to communicate, and if your volunteers can begin to understand their friends' unique ways of "talking" they can take their friendships to a deeper level.

Discussing the Details

Confidentiality

At times sensitive medical information, personal hygiene routines, or cognitive learning levels must be shared with the church, since it is essential to know these things in order to provide great care. This information must be handled with a high degree of confidentiality and respect. It can be a good idea for your volunteers to sign a confidentiality agreement as this helps to communicate the gravity of the issue and offers a level of accountability. This best practice standard provides the grounds to remind your volunteer of the agreement they signed if something is accidentally shared. Sensitive information should only be shared with those who need to know it for the care of that family. A volunteer might be well-intentioned in sharing information as a prayer request with their community group, but that may violate the trust of the family they are serving or embarrass their friend in some fashion. They way your volunteers handle confidential information is part of how they communicate love and respect to the families served by your ministry.

Communication

Along with confidentiality, it is good for your volunteers to know who they should communicate with when they want to share a story of how they see God working in their friend, discuss a practical need that arises, or seek counsel if a situation occurs that requires conversation with parents, caretakers or church staff. Regardless of the situation, it is helpful for volunteers to know who to approach. We generally recommend having volunteers communicate directly with whoever is in leadership over them. The leadership of your ministry can determine who should be involved in conversations and when it is appropriate to publicly share an encouraging story of the ministry.

Policies and Procedures

It is a good practice to make sure your volunteers are aware of the existing policies and procedures of your church. If your church does not have a policy on any of the below subjects, we recommend checking with your church's insurance company for sample policies.

- *Medical/hygiene policy* – This would include topics like toileting procedures, administering first aid, handling bodily discharges, seizures, violent behavior, and 911 calling protocol.
- *The check-in/out process for both the buddy and their friend* – It can also be helpful to address what to do if a friend runs away and gets lost, contacting parents in case of an emergency, and defining what constitutes an emergency.
- *Incident Report Policy* – Should an incident occur (i.e. an injury, abusive behavior, etc.) a procedure should be in place on who to inform and how they should be informed.
- *Fire and inclement weather procedures* – If you have friends attending class on the second floor who

use wheelchairs, or could not make it down the stairs without help, make sure you go over your evacuation plan for those individuals in case of an emergency.

Conclusion

As you wrap up your training session please do not forget to thank your volunteers. Remember that in serving they are giving their most precious resource – their time. As they invest their time in your ministry and make a lasting difference we pray that they too will be richly blessed by their experience.

Shadow-Style Training

Shadow-style training allows you to equip volunteers during your regular weekend services. It is best used when one or a few volunteers are joining your ministry and you do not have the time or need to host a large group training event. This style of training is not as efficient as large group trainings, but it can be highly effective as it allows you to personalize the training with your new recruit and build a relationship with them as you work together.

The teacher in shadow-style training can be you, someone on your leadership team or a volunteer who has served as a buddy for some time. We recommend doing shadow-style training over three to four weeks. Below is a sample schedule:

- **WEEK 1** – The new volunteer meets briefly with the teacher. At this time, the teacher should share with them a printed copy of essential information such as your ministry policies, emergency procedures, and the contact information of leadership. It is not necessary to walk them through the information—they can read it on their own time. The volunteer should bring a signature page acknowledging their agreement with the policies and procedures to you the following week. This week the volunteer should shadow the teacher simply observing and having limited involvement with their friend. They can take notes and have questions ready to discuss with their teacher the following week.

- **WEEK 2** – The new volunteer should bring the signature page acknowledging their agreement to the policies and procedures of your ministry. We recommend that receiving this signature page is required for them to continue with the second week of training. Once the signature page is received, the teacher can address any questions the volunteer has from the previous week. This week the new volunteer should take the lead with their friend while the teacher shadows and observes. The teacher should step in only when the volunteer has questions or needs help.

- **WEEK 3** – The new volunteer will take the lead independently. The teacher remains in the room and is available if the volunteer needs help, but at this point the volunteer is ready to serve their friend on their own.

- A fourth week can be added at any point in this process if additional training is needed.

Throughout the 3-4 weeks of training the teacher should be intentional to touch on specific topics described in the large group training section such as addressing behavior challenges, sharing Christ, and disability etiquette. As the teacher serves the friend assigned to them, the new volunteer will learn from his or her example.

However you decide to train your volunteers, the fact that you have taken the time to pour into them and equip them will give them the confidence and tools that they need to serve in your ministry with excellence.

Coaching Game Changers

When I was growing up, my family watched and played a lot of tennis. I spent many hours taking lessons and practicing. As I got into high school and the competition got harder I was very grateful for the years I had spent in practice. But it also became apparent that against some opponents all that time spent in practice was not enough. I knew the rules of the game, had drilled my strokes, and learned techniques. But if I lost too many games in a row I began to battle nervousness and frustration. If I was not careful, I would find myself losing because of unforced errors. I knew the battle was in my mind, and I was the one making the mistakes, yet it was difficult for me to identify that in the middle of the match. It was in those moments that my coach would counsel me, giving me pointers and suggestions on how to correct my errors. Whether or not I ended up winning the match my playing improved, I made less unforced errors, and I could walk off the court knowing I had done my best. As I recall those matches I realize that I never could have played my best without my coach. He challenged me, encouraged me and ultimately he was there when I needed him.

Leading the volunteers in your ministry is similar to how a coach leads the players on his or her team. Your volunteers need opportunities for growth, encouragement, and a coach who is available when they need help.

Coaching Through Opportunities for Growth

For many years there was a volunteer at Joni and Friends—let's call her Lynn. Lynn had been serving the ministry longer than many staff members had been employed. Because of the length and faithfulness of her service it was not unusual to hear staff members joke with her about taking some time off! Lynn faithfully served for so many years largely because she loves the ministry, but also because she knew her unique gifts and talents filled a need. Because of the longevity of her service, she was given greater levels of responsibility. This responsibility communicated to Lynn that we trusted her, that we valued her and that she was an important member of our team.

Can you remember a time when you were faced with a challenge? Maybe it was a hard project at work that you were not sure how to tackle, becoming a first-time parent, learning a language or recovering from a surgery. Do you remember how you felt once you overcame that challenge and gained confidence in that area? I can distinctly remember starting my first full time job. I had recently graduated college, gotten married, moved to a new state, and started full time work. At first the combination of these factors felt overwhelming, but after a few months I realized, "I am actually doing this and enjoying myself!" In successfully surviving my first few months in a new city with new responsibilities, I gained a confidence that has served me well both in my professional and personal life. For most people, having the opportunity to learn and gain competency in a new area is a rewarding experience. Growing in any capacity— whether personally, professionally, or spiritually—is part of what makes life rich.

This is true for volunteers as well. Having the opportunity to grow and develop new skills makes the experience of volunteering gratifying and fulfilling.

I encourage you to think about how you can offer your volunteers opportunities to learn new skills. Volunteers who start as a buddy for a friend could eventually become a trainer for new volunteers. A volunteer who helps with the check-in/pick-up process could begin helping with the snacks as well. Some volunteers may even be the right fit to begin helping with the scheduling of other volunteers within your ministry. You will certainly have some individuals who are delighted to serve in one role for some time and have very little interest in expanding their responsibility. However, I also feel confident that you will have volunteers who are hungry to get more involved and increase their level of ownership as they serve. There may also be times where you see a volunteer's potential and approach them with an opportunity for growth without them seeking it out. Taking time to think about a path for "promotion" will allow you to have a ready answer for volunteers who come to you excited to do more.

While exciting, growth opportunities can also be difficult and intimidating—both for the volunteer and for the ministry leader. The leader will probably need to let go of responsibilities and trust his or her volunteers to handle new responsibilities well.

The volunteer will need to learn new skills and be stretched outside of their comfort zone. This is like the football coach who has been watching the new recruit in practice—he sees talent in the young man but has not yet seen him play in a game. During the next game the coach decides to create an opportunity for growth and coach his player through it. By being in the game the player will have the opportunity to learn both on the field and after the game as the coach reviews the game films with him. The coach has taken a risk by putting him in the game, but he believes the risk will pay off by allowing the player to improve and eventually become a game changer.

You can also initiate growth for your volunteers by providing them with opportunities to speak into the ministry. Your volunteers are the ones who will be serving on the front lines week in and week out. They will probably be the first to notice areas of the ministry that are strong and areas that are weak. If you give them the time and place to share their ideas for the ministry, I would be surprised if you did not get some great feedback. While it will probably not be feasible for you to implement every idea that your volunteers share with you, it is important to take their ideas seriously and put into action the suggestions that you think could bless the ministry. Taking action based on a volunteer's suggestion will show your volunteers how much you value them, their service and their input in the special needs ministry. The old adage *actions speak louder than words* is very true in this context.

As you give your volunteers opportunities to increase their responsibility and speak into the ministry you will need to walk alongside your volunteers, giving them pointers, advice and encouragement. You are ultimately the coach of this team and should provide the overall plan and strategy on how to work as a unit influencing others for Christ.

Coaching Through Encouragement

As your volunteers learn the ins and outs of your ministry, they will doubtless make some mistakes and need occasional course correction. As they expand their roles and learn how to manage new responsibilities they will probably need continued guidance. A good coach knows when to correct and instruct, but a good coach also knows when to encourage and say thank you.

Last year I met at a coffee shop with a woman who teaches physical education classes to individuals affected by disability at a public school. She had recently started a special needs ministry at her local church and shared with me her feelings of discouragement about getting the ministry up and running. Towards the end of our conversation, I looked her in the eyes and said, "Thank you so much for all that you are doing to serve this community. You are doing a tremendous job and I have no doubt that you are making a huge difference for those children and their families!" I could visibly see her face and posture lift. She came to Starbucks feeling scattered and discouraged, but when we parted ways she left feeling excited and purposeful. It is amazing how a simple expression of gratitude and encouragement can make a significant impact.

We encourage ministry leaders to thank their volunteers consistently, creatively and candidly, placing equal importance on each aspect of that "gratitude motto."

- *Consistently* – Thanking your volunteers on a regular basis allows an atmosphere of appreciation to embody your ministry. If you are taking the time to express your gratitude consistently, your volunteers will have no reason to wonder if their hard work is being noticed. I personally try to make it a habit to say thank you to the volunteers that I work with every time I see them. We show them appreciation in other ways throughout the year as well, but saying "thank you for being here today!" is easy to do and helps them understand that their regular and faithful service is valued.

- *Creatively* – You can thank your volunteers a hundred different ways and barely scratch the surface. If you need creative help jump online and do a quick search—there are a myriad of fun ideas on how to say thank you to your volunteers. I recently found a great template online that said "Thanks a *latte* for all that you do!" I printed this out, attached a $5 coffee shop gift card to it, and gave it to volunteers as a way to show our appreciation. One local Southern California church prints T-shirts for their volunteers once a year with a new design. Their volunteers wear this T-shirt when they serve in the special needs ministry (and any other time they want to represent the ministry). It allows them to feel like they belong and it communicates that they are appreciated. Holding an annual appreciation luncheon can be a great way to honor your volunteers and bless them with a meal to say thank you. At a luncheon like this you could invite the senior pastor to address your volunteers, present them with a small gift, and give them the chance to fellowship with each other. If a larger event like that is not within your budget there are many simple ways to show your appreciation as well, like a handwritten thank you note or taking time to pray for them. Other ideas of showing gratitude could include a nice bar of chocolate, a birthday card, or finding ways to publicly thank them. Just remember that some volunteers do not like public recognition, so exercise this mode of gratitude wisely.

- *Candidly* – Saying thank you without meaning it is like giving someone a box of chocolates with one bite out of each chocolate. Something that is meant to bring joy can instead lead the recipient to feel frustrated and bitter—at least those are the feelings that rise up in me when I think about someone not being genuine or eating my chocolate! If you are ever feeling like frustration and weariness are keeping you from being genuine in your gratitude, pause and remember that volunteers are a gift. They do not have to be there and yet they choose to give their time, energy and talents to help the ministry grow. Telling your volunteers *why* you are thankful for them makes your message of appreciation authentic and can have much greater impact. It makes your "thank you" personal, showing that you notice your volunteers and what they do specifically to bless the ministry.

In addition to thanking your volunteers consistently, creatively and candidly I also suggest you make it a practice to share with them how their work is encouraging and uplifting the families they serve. This can be especially important for volunteers who are helping with administrative responsibilities and do not readily see the results of their efforts. When your volunteers share stories with you about how they saw God at work through their service, remember those stories and tell them to other volunteers as an encouragement of how their willingness to serve is changing lives.

For example, a volunteer at the headquarters of Joni and Friends may help with a mailing to donors.

This mailing may prompt a donor to give a gift that allows us to sponsor a family to attend Family Retreat or to purchase one or more wheelchairs for individuals overseas. Because of a volunteer's willingness to help serve, individuals will be exposed to the hope and truth of Jesus Christ through a Family Retreat or Wheels for the World outreach! Similarly, a volunteer serving at a respite event open to the public may have such profound influence on a child that when his or her parents come to pick them up they decide they would like to begin attending that church.

Understanding the full scope of how your time and efforts make an impact for the Kingdom of Christ is motivating and inspiring. Encouraging your volunteers in this manner can move them just as much or more than thank you cards or a special appreciation lunch. Volunteers who know that their leader appreciates and values them will typically give more as they serve, and will also get more in the way of satisfaction and enjoyment through their service.

Being a Coach Who Is Available

In my first year of employment with Joni and Friends I was given the opportunity to serve as a Short Term

Missionary (STM) at a Joni and Friends Family Retreat. I had never served as a buddy for a special needs ministry before and had nerves mingled with excitement as I read the profile of the family that I would be serving. In the first day or two of serving I had moments of feeling totally inadequate. I was so grateful that the woman who was serving as STM Coordinator for the week had made herself available to all of the STMs throughout the week. I was able to go to her with questions, insecurities and stories of success. She gave wise counsel, encouraged me and applauded my service. In all our conversations though, what I appreciated most was the fact that she was available. As I was learning my role I knew that I was not alone and that I was part of a bigger team working to make my assigned family feel welcomed, loved and rested.

You will most likely have volunteers who vary in their level of need for a coach's availability. Some volunteers will spread their wings and fly without looking back after training; others will probably want to check in with you throughout their first month or two of serving before feeling confident. Knowing that you are behind them and that you are accessible will give your volunteers an added level of confidence as they serve individuals and families affected by disability.

As volunteers turn to you with questions, you should try to be as informed as possible regarding the policies of your church and various situations that may arise. It is also important to know who you can turn to for answers when you are not sure of the answer yourself. In an attempt to help you feel more prepared as the leader of a special needs ministry, we have compiled a list of potential questions that new volunteers may ask. Found in the online appendices, this list includes questions like, "My friend shared something with me that I am concerned about. What do I do?" and, "What do I do if my friend runs away and I cannot find them?"

The answers for many of those questions will be specific to your church and the existing policies in place for the children's ministry. Many volunteers just need to hear that they should treat their friend like any other child. They need to hear that they should simply be kind and considerate, have fun and just be themselves! As is true with any child, it typically takes time to build a friendship. As your volunteers serve their friends week after week they will learn their likes, dislikes and habits. You can also encourage your volunteers to connect with the parents or caretakers of their friends. Parents and caretakers will know best the likes and dislikes of their child and how to most effectively communicate with them. Having your volunteers check in with the parents and caretakers of their friends will not only provide valuable information to your volunteers, but it will also show the parents and caretakers that your volunteers are invested in the wellbeing of their children.

As the leader of your ministry you should be your volunteers' best resource and their biggest cheerleader!

While being a good coach requires availability, being a good coach also requires being healthy. We recognize that most ministry leaders are stretched thin and barely have time to finish a cup of coffee while it is hot. We want to encourage you to do all that you can to support your volunteers and actively lead them, but we also want to encourage you to have boundaries. Being a coach who is available does not mean answering your phone any day, at any time. It does not mean that you need to fill in every time a volunteer cancels at the last minute. In order for you to serve your ministry and your volunteers with excellence and longevity, you will need to establish a pattern in your service that allows you to rest. How you find rest will be unique to you, but we highly recommend instituting some of the following practices:

- *Substitution Policy* - If you try to coordinate every cancellation and schedule change you will probably begin to feel frazzled and weary. We recommend distributing a schedule of all your volunteers and their contact information. If a volunteer has been scheduled for a shift and then needs to cancel, they should do their best to get that shift covered by calling other volunteers directly to find a replacement, and then communicating appropriately with the ministry leader.

- *Train up other leaders* - Identify several volunteers who can become your co-leaders. Bring them in on decisions and allow them to take ownership of the ministry alongside you. Having the ministry dependent on any one person opens the door for burnout and limits the longevity of the ministry.

- *Take time off* - Have Sundays where you do not serve in the special needs ministry so you can attend the mainstream Sunday service with your family or friends. If you are leading respite events limit the number you do in a year or occasionally allow other volunteers in the ministry to plan it. It is important for you to be personally refreshed and encouraged. Taking a step back can allow you to see the impact of your ministry rather than focusing on all the to-dos and details.

- *Practice saying no in other areas* - If you are committing to leading or being on a leadership team for a special needs ministry you will have a full schedule. To give your best to this ministry you will probably need to limit your other commitments. Over-committing generally results in weariness and an inability to be fully present.

While it may seem counterintuitive to make yourself an available coach by creating healthy boundaries, we strongly encourage you to try it! We also recognize that the principles set forth in this book could be a lot to tackle, especially if you are just starting your ministry. Please remember that the relationships you build with your volunteers are more important than making sure you have a perfect program. As a leader, if you are in a place where you feel rested and balanced you will be able to give more to your volunteers and to the ministry. It is wise to model healthy habits for your volunteers so they learn to create boundaries that allow them to serve with greater enthusiasm and longevity as well.

The Impact of
Game Changers

As you move through the process of recruiting, training and coaching your volunteers, our hope and prayer is that your ministry blossoms. I have worked with volunteers in varying capacities for many years, and I cannot count the lives that have been radically changed for Christ because of the efforts of those volunteers. It humbles me to recall the sacrifice of amazing individuals giving their time and energy to advance the work of ministries. I have seen ministries multiplied and accelerated because of volunteer labor. But as I reflect on these memories, I cannot help but be impressed with the impact that all of these volunteers have had on me personally. Because of these game changers I have been inspired and motivated. I have been given tangible examples of strength, selflessness, generosity, humility and inner beauty. My life has been enriched because of these individuals. For me, these volunteers have been game changers, and I was not even the recipient of their service.

Muriel was an older woman who served several days a week doing administrative work for Joni and Friends. Despite ongoing complications with her physical health she made it a priority to come and serve. She judiciously shared wisdom and encouragement with all the other volunteers and staff members. I recall being amazed and inspired as she shared with me her decision to serve for several years as a missionary in Russia after retiring from a lengthy teaching career. After serving with the mission agency in Russia, she returned to the US and spent many years serving as a full-time volunteer splitting her days between various churches and ministries. She served until the day the Lord called her home. I was greatly moved to look at the crowd of individuals who attended her memorial service—hundreds of people who had been blessed and inspired because of the quiet, faithful, generosity of a woman who regularly gave of herself and her time to bless those around her.

For all the practical advice that this booklet offers, our greatest hope is that you close this binding with a better understanding of the overall role volunteers play in your ministry. Recruiting, training and coaching volunteers will require an initial investment of time, but will bring strength and longevity to your ministry. Empowering volunteers will allow you, as the ministry leader, to pour into the families you serve on a deeper level. We encourage you to create an atmosphere that is attractive to volunteers—one that supports, encourages, pushes and celebrates volunteers. And we pray that as you engage, train, and coach these individuals that you will gain the ultimate winning advantage—that you, your volunteers and the families you are serving all grow closer to Christ and increase in passion for serving those affected by disabilities.

Becoming *Irresistible*

Luke 14 commands Christ followers to "Go quickly... find the blind, the lame, and the crippled...and compel them to come in!" While this sounds inspiring and daunting, exciting and overwhelming, motivating and frightening, all at the same time, what does it actually mean? How do we live and function within the church in such a way that families affected by disability are compelled to walk through our doors to experience the body of Christ?

We can certainly *compel* them by offering programs, ministries, events, and other church activities, but what if the compelling aspect was more about heart, culture, acceptance and embracing? What if our churches were overflowing with the hope of Jesus Christ...a hope not simply for those who "fit in" or look the part, but rather a hope to all, including the marginalized, downtrodden and outcast?

Becoming *Irresistible* is more than programs and activities—it is about a transformational work in our hearts...first as individuals and then as the body of Christ. *Irresistible* allows us to see each individual as he or she truly is: created in the image of God (Genesis 1:26-27), designed purposely as a masterpiece (Psalm 139:13-14), instilled with purpose, plans and dreams (Jeremiah 29:11), and a truly indispensable member of the kingdom of God (1 Corinthians 12:23). An *Irresistible Church* is an "authentic community built on the hope of Christ that compels people affected by disability to fully belong." It is powerful for a person to know that he or she is fully welcomed and belongs. *Irresistible* captures the heart of the church as it should be—how else do we explain the rapid growth and intense attraction to the church in the book of Acts? The heart of God was embodied through the people of God by the Spirit of God...and that is simply *Irresistible*!

The Irresistible Church Series is designed to help not only shape and transform the heart of the church, but also to provide the practical steps and activities to put *flesh* around the *heart* of the church—to help your church become a place for people to fully belong. Thank you for responding to the call to become *Irresistible*. It will not happen overnight, but it will happen. As with all good things, it requires patience and perseverance, determination and dedication, and ultimately an underlying trust in the faithfulness of

God. May God bless you on this journey. Be assured that you are not alone—there are many on the path of *Irresistible*.

For more information or to join the community, please visit www.irresistiblechurch.org.

Joni and Friends
INTERNATIONAL DISABILITY CENTER

Joni and Friends was established in 1979 by Joni Eareckson Tada, who at 17 was injured in a diving accident, leaving her a quadriplegic. Since its inception, Joni and Friends has been dedicated to extending the love and message of Christ to people who are affected by disability whether it is the disabled person, a family member, or friend. Our objective is to meet the physical, emotional, and spiritual needs of this group of people in practical ways.

Joni and Friends is committed to recruiting, training, and motivating new generations of people with disabilities to become leaders in their churches and communities. Today, the Joni and Friends International Disability Center serves as the administrative hub for an array of programs which provide outreach to thousands of families affected by disability around the globe. These include two radio programs, an award-winning television series, the Wheels for the World international wheelchair distribution ministry, Family Retreats which provide respite for those with disabilities and their families, Field Services to provide church training along with educational and inspirational resources at a local level, and the Christian Institute on Disability to establish a firm biblical worldview on disability-related issues.

From local neighborhoods to the far reaches of the world, Joni and Friends is striving to demonstrate to people affected by disability, in tangible ways, that God has not abandoned them—he is with them—providing love, hope, and eternal salvation.

Available Now in the Irresistible Church Series

Start with Hello
Introducing Your Church to Special Needs Ministry

Families with special needs often share that they desire two things in their church: accessibility and acceptance. Accessibility to existing structures, programs and people is an imperative. Acceptance with a sense of belonging by the others who also participate in the structures, programs and fellowship of the church is equally necessary. In this simple book you'll learn the five steps to becoming an accessible and accepting church.

To receive first notice of upcoming resources, including respite, inclusive worship and support groups, please contact us at churchrelations@joniandfriends.org.

Available Now in the Irresistible Church Series

We've Got This!
Providing Respite for Families Affected by Disability

Families or caregivers who have children with disabilities are often isolated, exhausted, and grieving. Respite events can be a safe bridge for families to cross over the threshold of the church by satisfying an urgent need. A place for children to be themselves, for caregivers to have a break and for the church to serve well is invaluable. This book is a practical guide that provides the necessary tools to plan and execute a successful respite event.

To receive first notice of upcoming resources, including respite, inclusive worship and support groups, please contact us at churchrelations@joniandfriends.org.

Other Recommended Resources

Beyond Suffering® ***Classic Edition***	***Beyond Suffering®*** ***Student Edition***	***Joni:*** ***An Unforgettable Story***

Beyond Suffering: A Christian View on Disability Ministry provides you with a roadmap to an effective and inspiring disability ministry. *Beyond Suffering* is a comprehensive course that gives an overview of the theological and practical underpinnings of the movement. It will equip you to think critically, compassionately and clearly about the complex issues that impact people with disabilities and their families and to confidently bring them the love of Christ.

ISBN: 978-0-9838484-0-0
272 pages · 8.5" x 11"
Includes CD-ROM

Beyond Suffering for the Next Generation: A Christian View on Disability Ministry will equip young people to consider the issues that affect people with disabilities and their families, and inspire them to action. Students who embrace this study will gain confidence to join a growing, worldwide movement that God is orchestrating to fulfill Luke 14:21-23: "Go out quickly into the streets and alleys of the town and bring in the poor, the crippled, the blind, and the lame.... so that my house will be full."

ISBN: 978-0-9838484-6-2
304 pages · 8.5" x 11"
Includes CD-ROM

In this unforgettable autobiography, Joni reveals each step of her struggle to accept her disability and discover the meaning of her life. The hard-earned truths she discovers and the special ways God reveals his love are testimonies to faith's triumph over hardship and suffering. This new edition includes an afterword, in which Joni talks about the events that have occurred in her life since the book's original publication in 1976, including her marriage and the expansion of her worldwide ministry to families affected by disability.

ISBN: 978-0310240013
205 pages · Paperback

www.joniandfriends.org · P.O. Box 3333, Agoura Hills, CA 91376
(818) 707-5664 · Fax: (818) 707-2391 TTY: (818) 707-9707

Customizable Resources from the Book

Available for Download at
http://www.joniandfriends.org/church-relations/

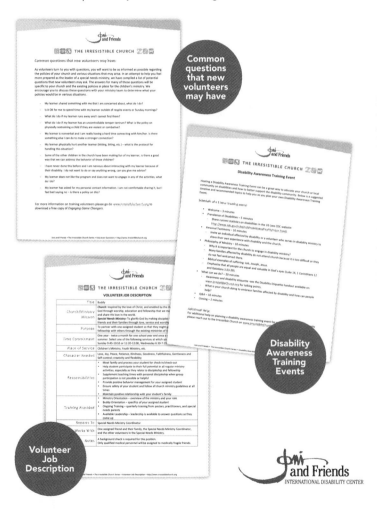

Common questions that new volunteers may have

Disability Awareness Training Events

Volunteer Job Description